IELTS SPEAKING PART 1 STRATEGIES

The Ultimate Guide With Tips, Tricks, And Practice On How To Get A Target Band Score Of 8.0+ In 10 Minutes A Day

RACHEL MITCHELL

Copyright © 2017

All rights reserved.

ISBN: 9781549719882

TEXT COPYRIGHT © [RACHEL MITCHELL]

all rights reserved. No part of this guide may be reproduced in any form without permission in writing from the publisher except in the case of brief quotations embodied in critical articles or reviews.

Legal & disclaimer

The information contained in this book and its contents is not designed to replace or take the place of any form of medical or professional advice; and is not meant to replace the need for independent medical, financial, legal or other professional advice or services, as may be required. The content and information in this book have been provided for educational and entertainment purposes only.

The content and information contained in this book have been compiled from sources deemed reliable, and it is accurate to the best of the author's knowledge, information, and belief. However, the author cannot guarantee its accuracy and validity and cannot be held liable for any errors and/or omissions. Further, changes are periodically made to this book as and when needed. Where appropriate and/or necessary, you must consult a professional (including but not limited to your doctor, attorney, financial advisor or such other professional advisor) before using any of the suggested remedies, techniques, or information in this book.

Upon using the contents and information contained in this book, you agree to hold harmless the author from and against any damages, costs, and expenses, including any legal fees potentially resulting from the application of any of the information provided by this book. This disclaimer applies to any loss, damages or injury caused by the use and application, whether directly or indirectly, of any advice or information presented, whether for breach of contract, tort, negligence, personal injury, criminal intent, or under any other cause of action.

You agree to accept all risks of using the information presented inside this book.

You agree that by continuing to read this book, where appropriate and/or necessary, you shall consult a professional (including but not limited to your doctor, attorney, or financial advisor or such other advisor as needed) before using any of the suggested remedies, techniques, or information in this book.

TABLE OF CONTENT

Introduction
IELTS Speaking Introduction
Part 1 Speaking Topics
What Will Give You A High Score In The Speaking Part 1?
How Does The Examiner Mark Your Speaking Test?
Part 1 Speaking Essentials
Fluency Markers
Time and Frequency Expressions
Adverbials for Giving Opinions
Part 1 Speaking Practice
Preference Questions
Part 1 Speaking Model Answers
List Of Part 1 Speaking Questions To Practice At Home
Conclusion
Check Out Other Books

INTRODUCTION

Thank you and congratulate you for downloading the book *"IELTS Speaking Part 1 Strategies: The Ultimate Guide with Tips, Tricks and Practice on How to Get a Target Band Score of 8.0+ in 10 Minutes a Day."*

This book is well designed and written by an experienced native teacher from the USA who has been teaching IELTS for over 10 years. She really is the expert in training IELTS for students at each level. In this book, she will provide you all proven Formulas, Tips, Tricks, Strategies, Explanations, Structures, Part 1 Speaking Language, Vocabulary and Model Part 1 Answers to help you easily achieve an 8.0+ in the IELTS Part 1 Speaking, even if your speaking is not excellent. This book will also walk you through step-by-step on how to develop your well-organized answers for the Part 1 Speaking; clearly analyze and explains the different types of questions that are asked for Part 1 Speaking; provide you step-by-step instructions on how to answer each type of question excellently.

As the author of this book, Rachel Mitchell believes that this book will be an indispensable reference and trusted guide for you who may want to maximize your band score in IELTS Part 1 Speaking. Once you read this book, I guarantee you that you will have learned an extraordinarily wide range of useful, and practical IELTS Part 1 Speaking strategies and formulas that will help you become a successful IELTS taker as well as you will even become a successful English user in work and in life within a short period of time only.

Take action today and start getting better scores tomorrow!

Thank you again for purchasing this book, and I hope you enjoy it.

IELTS SPEAKING INTRODUCTION

The IELTS speaking test lasts about 11 to 14 minutes. It has 3 parts, and it's worth 25% of your IELTS score.

However, the speaking test is very unique because it's much shorter than the other sections. Specifically, writing test (1 hour), listening test (45 minutes), reading (1 hour), and speaking test (11-14 minutes).

The IELTS speaking test is shorter but it gives you more opportunities to practice more basic skills.

Let's talk about the three parts of the speaking test.

PART 1 SPEAKING TOPICS

The skills in part 1 speaking are exactly the skills that we need for part 2 and part 3 speaking. So what we need to do in part 1 speaking is we need to focus on building basic skills.

There are two purposes to part 1 speaking. The first purpose is to calm you down. They know that you are nervous, so they're going to ask you simple questions that get you settle down and prepare for part 2 & part 3 speaking (the more difficult parts). The second purpose of part 1 speaking is of course for you to show the examiner your ability to speak English. They want you to calm down and they want you to show the most you can do with your English.

In part 1 speaking, the questions are about **you, your home, your life, your family, or your country**, which are things that you have the answer to. They are not asking you questions like *"who wants to be a billionaire?"*, *"who was the 15th president of the United States?"*. Normally, in part 1 speaking, they will be giving you 3 topics:

The 1st topic: The first topic will always be *"do you work or do you study?"* or *"where you are living?"*

If you answer that you are working, then they will ask you about your work.

If you answer that you are studying, then they will ask you about your study.

The next 2nd and 3rd topics: The next 2nd and 3rd topics can be about **anything**, but it is not going to be a sensitive topic; they are not going to ask you about politics. Instead, they will ask you something about general topics that you have ideas to answer. These things might be about **rain,** for example, *how often does it rain in your country?* Or *how do you feel when it rains?*. They also might ask you questions about **movies, colors, hobbies, etc**. These are simple questions, they are not challenging questions, but we cannot easily predict what the examiner will be asking you about.

Here is the thing. The examiner doesn't care about your answer. If they ask you *"do you like to read?"* they don't care if you say *"yes, I love reading"* or *"no, I hate it"*. They don't care, they want to hear *how you communicate*.

WHAT WILL GIVE YOU A HIGH SCORE IN THE SPEAKING PART 1?

Rule Number 1: Answer the question. Make sure you answer the question.

For example: *do you like to read books?*

Well, books are really enjoyable. People like to read books because they find it very relaxing, and they can get a lot of information from books. My father really enjoys reading; and every Friday night, he sits at home with a book and drinks some tea….

Am I answering the question? **No, I am not.**

Definitely, the examiner does know that I did not answer the question because I chose not to. I didn't answer the question.

Rule Number 2: you need to show the examiner something or some things about your English ability, and that can be something about your grammar, something about your vocabulary, something about the organization of your answer, and maybe something about your pronunciation.

We must know that IELTS is a game, and a test is a method with rules that allows you to gain points and lose points. Therefore, in order to be successful with any game and IELTS in particular, we need to know what the rules are, and we need to know how to gain points, **not** lose points.

Example: *"Do you enjoy reading?"*

Answer 1: *Yes, I love to read*

Answer 2: *To be honest, I hate reading. I think it's a stupid hobby. I think people that read are actually very boring and they annoy me tremendously.*

Which answer is better? The first one or the second one? Of course, the second one. Even though the second answer is a bit strange, a bit rude, but that's not what the examiner will mark in the IELTS exam. Good vocabulary, good grammar, good sentence structures; that is what they mark. So, show the examiner your English ability.

Note that **never** give a one-word answer, always use complete sentences or at least complete phrases, and extend your answer by providing some kinds of explanations or descriptions.

For example: *"Do you enjoy reading?"*

Answer: ***"yes"***

Well, if you just give a one-word answer like this, you've got nothing with your pronunciation, nothing with your vocabulary, and nothing with your grammar. You've got nothing.

What you need to do is you need to extend your answer. The big mistake of part 1 speaking that a lot of people make is that they lose sight over how important it is. In fact, speaking part 1 is quite easy. However, most people tend to expect something more difficult in part 1 speaking such as, *"please get me the harder questions? Or "please get me the good questions?"*. But **no**, the questions they give you in part 1 speaking are already the good stuff, and you will see that the way you answer questions in part 1 speaking is exactly what you need for part 2 and part 3 speaking. Therefore, you need to be willing to practice questions for part 1 speaking.

HOW DOES THE EXAMINER MARK YOUR SPEAKING TEST?

You need to know and understand the four categories. Let's take a look at the IELTS speaking band descriptors as below:

IELTS Speaking band descriptors (public version)

Band	Fluency and Coherence	Lexical Resource	Lexical Resource	Pronunciation
9	• speaks fluently with only rare repetition or self correction; any hesitation is content-related rather than to find words or grammar • speaks coherently with fully appropriate cohesive features • develops topics fully and appropriately	• uses vocabulary with full flexibility and precision in all topics • uses idiomatic language naturally and accurately	• uses a full range of structures naturally and appropriately • produces consistently accurate structures apart from 'slips' characteristic of native speaker speech	• uses a full range of pronunciation features with precision and subtlety • sustains flexible use of features throughout • is effortless to understand
8	• speaks fluently with only occasional repetition or self-correction; hesitation is usually content-related and only rarely to search for language • develops topics coherently and appropriately	• uses a wide vocabulary resource readily and flexibly to convey precise meaning • uses less common and idiomatic vocabulary skilfully, with occasional inaccuracies • uses paraphrase effectively as required	• uses a wide range of structures flexibly • produces a majority of error-free sentences with only very occasional inappropriacies or basic/non-systematic errors	• uses a wide range of pronunciation features • sustains flexible use of features, with only occasional lapses • is easy to understand throughout; L1 accent has minimal effect on intelligibility
7	• speaks at length without noticeable effort or loss of coherence • may demonstrate language-related hesitation at times, or some repetition and/or self-correction • uses a range of connectives and discourse markers with some flexibility	• uses vocabulary resource flexibly to discuss a variety of topics • uses some less common and idiomatic vocabulary and shows some awareness of style and collocation, with some inappropriate choices • uses paraphrase effectively	• uses a range of complex structures with some flexibility • frequently produces error-free sentences, though some grammatical mistakes persist	• shows all the positive features of Band 6 and some, but not all, of the positive features of Band 8
6	• is willing to speak at length, though may lose coherence at times due to occasional repetition, self-correction or hesitation • uses a range of connectives and discourse markers but not always appropriately	• has a wide enough vocabulary to discuss topics at length and make meaning clear in spite of inappropriacies • generally paraphrases successfully	• uses a mix of simple and complex structures, but with limited flexibility • may make frequent mistakes with complex structures, though these rarely cause comprehension problems	• uses a range of pronunciation features with mixed control • shows some effective use of features but this is not sustained • can generally be understood throughout, though mispronunciation of individual words or sounds reduces clarity at times

5	• usually maintains flow of speech but uses repetition, self-correction and/or slow speech to keep going • may over-use certain connectives and discourse markers • produces simple speech fluently, but more complex communication causes fluency problems	• manages to talk about familiar and unfamiliar topics but uses vocabulary with limited flexibility • attempts to use paraphrase but with mixed success	• produces basic sentence forms with reasonable accuracy • uses a limited range of more complex structures, but these usually contain errors and may cause some comprehension problems	• shows all the positive features of Band 4 and some, but not all, of the positive features of Band 6	
4	• cannot respond without noticeable pauses and may speak slowly, with frequent repetition and self-correction • links basic sentences but with repetitious use of simple connectives and some breakdowns in coherence	• is able to talk about familiar topics but can only convey basic meaning on unfamiliar topics and makes frequent errors in word choice • rarely attempts paraphrase	• produces basic sentence forms and some correct simple sentences but subordinate structures are rare • errors are frequent and may lead to misunderstanding	• uses a limited range of pronunciation features • attempts to control features but lapses are frequent • mispronunciations are frequent and cause some difficulty for the listener	
3	• speaks with long pauses • has limited ability to link simple sentences • gives only simple responses and is frequently unable to convey basic message	• uses simple vocabulary to convey personal information • has insufficient vocabulary for less familiar topics	• attempts basic sentence forms but with limited success, or relies on apparently memorised utterances • makes numerous errors except in memorised expressions	• shows some of the features of Band 2 and some, but not all, of the positive features of Band 4	
2	• pauses lengthily before most words • little communication possible	• only produces isolated words or memorised utterances	• cannot produce basic sentence forms	• speech is often unintelligible	
1	• no communication possible • no rateable language				
0	• does not attend				

1. **FLUENCY AND COHESION:** The first category that the examiner is marking your speaking is the fluency and cohesion. They will be marking you on:

- Do you speak <u>smoothly without long pauses</u>?
- Do you <u>produce new information</u>?
- Do you <u>link your ideas by using fluency markers</u>?

Fluency markers are words like *"however", "furthermore", "also", "as a result", "consequently", "so", "unfortunately", "for example",* etc.

You <u>should be fluent</u> not only in part 1 speaking, but also in part 2 and part 3 speaking.

Note that fluency **is not speed** (<u>not too fast</u> and <u>not too slow</u>). Unfortunately, some students are going to hurt their score when they try to speak too fast because their mouth is going too fast to their brain.

2. **LEXICAL RESOURCE (VOCABULARY):** The second category that we should think about is Lexical Resource. You will be doing a lot of

vocabularies in your IELTS speaking:

+ You should use **linking vocabulary**. You should use **words that signal** such as *therefore, so, for example, nowadays, unfortunately, surprisingly, etc.*

+ You should use **topic vocabulary**: vocabulary that we will use for particular topics, for example, *topics about television, movies and books, technology, etc.*

+ You should use **phrasal verbs** *such as, look into, look onto, etc.*

+ You should use a range of words. You **don't** just want to say *"it's really good"*, or *"it's good"*, or *"everything is good"*. You should make your answer better by using a range of synonym words of *"good"*. You can use *"fantastic/ spectacular/awesome/tremendous, etc."*

+ You will not get a high score unless you use a wide range of vocabulary accurately, and you do some simple things like *"paraphrasing"*. **Paraphrasing** is when you change the words that they ask you in the question. For example, if they ask you *"do you like to read?"* You **should not** say *"yes, I love to read."* Although your grammar is ok, but if you want to get a better score you **should say** *"yes, I love reading"*. Certainly, you will get a better score because you have changed the verb form. Or you can say *"yes, I love doing that"*.

When you start to learn vocabulary words, it's really good to build vocabulary as you keep going, as you keep studying, but you don't have to sit down and try to study about 20 vocabulary words. Instead of doing that, it's better if you try to only learn may be 1 or 2 words at a time, and then immediately start using the words. Don't learn a list of 10 words, and then think *"oh, I've just learnt the 10 words"*. You shouldn't do that. What you should do is to learn 2 words a day and start using those words right away by using those words often in sentences, then you will find that you learn words more deeply, and the more you do it, the quicker your brain processes new vocabulary.

Idioms: The other thing you should do if you want to get a higher score (7.0+) is that you need to be able to use a range of **idioms**. Idioms are phrases that don't mean exactly what they sound what they mean, for example, *"raining cats and dogs"*, *"become green with envy"*, *"cost an arm and a leg"*, *"sleep like a baby"*. **Idioms** are very challenging, and this is the one thing that almost students do not use in the final test. Why? Remember that when the examiner asks you certain questions, they are inviting certain answers. For example, if they ask you *"would you like to travel to another country?"*

Note that, if the examiner asks you a question with the modal verb *"would"*, they are inviting you to give them an answer using a modal verb back, but there are no questions that the examiner asks you to give them an idiom. You have to <u>create the opportunity to use idioms</u>. You have to be confident enough in your English, quick enough with your vocabulary to be able to use idioms properly.

Use idiomatic expressions and phrasal verbs for accurate collocations. The best way to learn phrases is **reading**. Reading will help you learn idiomatic expressions and phrasal verbs for accurate collocations effectively. Reading will help you improve your writing score, listening score, and even your speaking score. These are things that you need to be aware of.

I don't expect you to learn all of English idioms. I only expect you to learn a handle of them (5-6-7-8 idioms) that you know perfectly; that you think you are able to use them perfectly in the exam.

The use of idioms is a high-level skill. Using them properly, not overusing them.

Try to paraphrase as much as you can and use idioms in your speaking. Use fluency markers that you talk about.

You can boost your vocabulary by using paraphrasing, using idioms and you can improve your pronunciation. You can get up to 7.0+ with your pronunciation in 3 months if you practice your pronunciation every day.

<u>LIST OF USEFUL IDIOMS:</u>

It's as easy as pie = it's a piece of cake: to be very easy, (not complicated).

- I don't think <u>it's as easy as pie</u> to get band 8.5 in the IELTS speaking test.
- <u>It's a piece of cake</u> to drive this car.

Cost an arm and a leg: to be very expensive.

- *The movie is interesting, but the tickets cost an arm and a leg.*
- *The car cost him an arm and a leg.*

Pay through the nose: to pay too much for something.

- *I usually have to pay through the nose for parking a car if I bring it into the city.*
- *He paid through the nose to get the car fixed.*

Make someone blue = bump someone out: to make someone sad or sick.

- *It made him blue to have to stay home with his wife all day.*
- *He made his girlfriend blue yesterday.*

Freak out: to become very angry or lose control of your mind because of somebody or something.

- *I freaked out when I saw her with another man.*
- *Snakes really freaked me out.*

In the nick of time: just before it's too late/ at the last possible moment.

- *We got to the airport just in the nick of time.*
- *I arrived at the train station in the nick of time.*
- *She finished her English essay just in the nick of time.*

It's raining cats and dogs: it's raining a lot/ it is raining heavily.

- *It's windy and is raining cats and dogs.*
- *It was raining cats and dogs, so all flights were delayed.*

(Like) two peas in a pod: very similar, especially in appearance.

- Peter and his brother are *like two peas in a pod*.
- The twins are *like two peas in a pod*.

(As) sly as a fox: someone who is clever, cunning, wily, and tricky.

- Many people don't like him because he is *sly as a fox*.
- My boss is as *sly as a fox*.

Poke around: look around a place, typically in search of something (you can poke around on the internet, you can poke around on the streets, etc. to look for/search for something).

- Just *poke around* the Internet, you'll find a lot of dating websites.
- He *poked around* in his desk to see if the wallet was there.

Mean business: to be very, very serious.

- I thought he was joking at first, but then I saw that he really *meant business*.
- Just looking at him, I knew he *meant business*.

Hit the hay = hit the sack: to go to bed.

- I'm pretty tired. I think it's time for me to *hit the hay*.
- I'm going to *hit the sack* early since I've got to get up early tomorrow.

Sleep like a baby: to sleep very well; to sleep deeply.

- After a long, hard day at work, I *slept like a baby* last night.
- He was very tired, so he went to bed, and *slept like a baby*.

Once in a blue moon: very rarely/very seldom/almost never.

- My son lives in Canada and he only comes to see us *once in a blue moon*.
- My family used to live in Tokyo, but now we only go there *once in a blue moon*.

Ace a test: to do very well in a test/ to get a very high score on a test.

- *You need to study hard to <u>ace a test</u>.*

- *She had actually <u>aced a test</u> in Math, a subject that had never come easily for her.*

Ring a bell: to sound familiar.

- *The name Lucy doesn't <u>ring a bell</u>.*

- *I've never met Sarah, but her name <u>rings a bell</u>.*

Green with envy: to be jealous/ to be envious.

- *Tom was <u>green with envy</u> when he saw that I got a new car for my birthday.*

- *My expensive house makes him <u>green with envy</u>.*

Drive someone crazy: to make him or her upset or annoyed.

- *Tom quit his job because his boss <u>drove him crazy</u> every time he went to work.*

- *The constant noise <u>drove me crazy</u>.*

The cat that ate the canary: to look very happy/ very pleased.

- *He was smiling like <u>the cat that ate the canary</u>.*

- *You look like <u>the cat that ate the canary</u>.*

3. GRAMMAR:

Pay attention to a grammatical range of accuracy.

- *Are you making mistakes?*
- *How many mistakes are you making?*
- *Are those mistakes reducing the examiner's ability to be able to understand you?*

That's the key.

Forget about being perfect, you're not going to be perfect. Don't chase perfection, you never get it. So, what can you do? Well, I would say that you should focus on the big mistakes that you are making usually. Those are verb tenses, article and adjectives like *"I felt so bored* (not ~~boring~~). Something like that.

Another thing you need to pay your attention to is that subject-verb agreement.

My father has (not ~~have~~) a motorbike.

4. PRONUNCIATION

Pronunciation is probably the thing you use the most. The fact about pronunciation is that a lot of you need to know how badly it destroys your band score even though your grammar and vocabulary are good. It really does. It kills. So you need to spend time practicing your pronunciation. Pronunciation is by far the easiest thing for you to fix in your English.

Note that pronunciation is 100% physical.

What is a word?

A word is a collection of sounds. For example, the word "MIXED" is a collection of the sounds "M.I.K.S.T"

The problem is that you don't know where the sounds are, you don't know how to make the sounds and you don't do it enough. So try to **practice** your pronunciation enough.

How to be good at pronunciation?

One of the reasons my pronunciation is so clear is that I have focused years for years on finishing my sounds (li<u>ke</u>, becau<u>se</u>). My pronunciation is not accidentally clear, my pronunciation is clear by being designed because I am extremely precise with every sound that I have made. You can learn the same thing. It's not magic, it's not intelligent, it's just focused, focused and focused. You have to be precise, and you have to practice pronunciation often.

Work at it every day. Don't try to pronounce the words too fast.

PART 1 SPEAKING ESSENTIALS

What does the word **"essential"** mean? It means *"very important, highly critical, necessary"*

The skills that you learn for part 1 speaking are 100% the foundation of part 2 and part 3 speaking. If you do a poor job in part 1 speaking, the examiner will be supposed to give you just a 5.0 before you have done part 2 & part 3 speaking.

When it comes to part 1 speaking, I would say that you need to remember these things:

Number 1: **Never** answer with only one word. Always use complete sentences or phrases.

If they ask you *"do you like to read?"*

If you just say: *yes*

Well, your answer has no grammar, no pronunciation, no vocabulary. All they know is *"you like to read"*.

What is the better answer of *"do you like to read?"*

Answer: **Yes, I would love to…**

Or: ***no, reading is boring. I think that people who read are quite stupid. Frankly, I think they should be doing more fun things like motorbike racing or knife fighting…***

This answer is better. You might disagree because the answer sounds a bit rude, and it talks a lot about a bad lifestyle (motorbike racing, knife fighting). However, the examiner is not going to give you a band score based on how nice a person you are, they will give you a band score based on your English ability. So be sure that you give them what they want.

Number 2: you need to show the examiner something or some things about your English, and that can be something about your grammar, something about your vocabulary, something about the organization of your answer, and maybe something about your pronunciation.

For example, if they ask you *"do you like watching TV?"*

And you say: *of course, I love watching TV.*

When you say *"I love..."* you stressed the word ***"love"***. That means you've shown something about your pronunciation.

These are things you need to think about: answer the question and extend your answer. Show something about your English ability. For each question, try to produce your answer in different ways to show different things about your speaking. There are some basic things you can do right away. First of all, you add details by using those basic questions in English: *"who", "what", "when", "where", "why", "how", "how often", "how much", etc.*

So if they ask you *"do you like watching TV?"*

You can say: *Yes, I love watching TV. I really love Mr. Bean. He is my favorite TV character. I often watch TV with my family in the living room on the weekend.*

Or if they ask you *"do you like reading books?"*

You can say: *yes, I really love reading books mainly because it's so relaxing. I remember when I was in high school, my teacher gave me a really good book and inspired me to read more and more.*

Before answering the question, make sure you pay attention to the question type, the verb tense *("do you like to read?"* or *"did you like to read when you were a child?" Or "what book would you like to read?")*. Be careful about this.

For example: *"Do you like reading books?"*

What's the verb tense of this question? *Present tense.*

Answer: *Yes, I really love reading books mainly because it's so relaxing. I remember when I was in high school, my teacher gave me a really good book and inspired me to read more and more.*

Did I answer the question?

Yes, and then I switched from present tense to past tense. That is something else you can do. You can do a lot of things when it comes to extending your answer; you can use non-defining relative clauses to add extra information about anything you want to say. So think about this.

I can say *"I really enjoy reading comic books. These books are very entertaining."* (2 sentences)

But I can combine them and make 1 sentence by using a *non-defining relative clause*.

"I really love reading comic books, which are very entertaining."

Like I said, you can change the verb tense.

If they ask you *"did you enjoy reading books when you were a child?"*

What's the verb tense of this question? *Past tense*, right?

So, be sure you answer the question, but go ahead and switch the verb tense if you want.

You can say: *To be honest, I didn't really like reading so much when I was a kid. But nowadays, I'm pretty keen on reading mystery novels. Actually, I'm going to the bookstore after the class tonight, and I'll buy some mystery novels.*

So I just gave the examiner the answer using past tense, present tense and future tense.

You can use the adverbs of frequency. You can talk about how often or how rarely you do something. Use a range adverbs of frequency and be careful not just giving the adverb back to the examiner.

For example, if they ask you *"what do you usually do on the weekend?"*

You shouldn't say: *on the weekend, I usually*.

That's fine, proper grammar, but if you want to get a high score, you should change *"usually"* into *"frequently"* or *"often"*. You should paraphrase it.

Stay away from using 100% and 0% statement like *always, never*, etc.

Example 1: *"What do you do on the weekend?"*

Answer: *I ~~always~~ go to the mall and talk to everyone*

"Always go to the mall?" does this sound like accurate communication? *Is it possible to always go the mall every weekend?* That sounds a little **strange**.

Example 2: *"What do you do on the weekend?"*

Answer: *I ~~always~~ do my homework.*

Never have a weekend off? Always to 100% of the time on the weekend you do your homework? That doesn't sound like accurate.

Example 3: *"do you like fast food?"*

Answer: *To be honest, it's disgusting, I ~~never~~ eat it.*

Never eat fast food? That doesn't sound like accurate.

So I would say that you should be very careful of using these adverbs of frequency **always** and **never** in your answers.

Paraphrasing: you can use **synonyms** and **parallel expressions** to paraphrase the question in your answer.

For example, if they ask you *"what did you like to read as a child?"*

It's very easy to get into the bad habit if you say *"As a child, I ~~like to read~~."*

Your grammar is ok, however, your vocabulary score is low because you didn't show the examiner your vocabulary, you borrowed his vocabulary, and you used it in your answer.

So if they ask you *"what did you like to read as a child?"*

You should paraphrase your answer like *"when I was a kid, I love reading…"* it's much better.

Or you can say *"back then, I enjoyed reading…"*

"Back then" in this case means *"when I was a child"*

Or you can <u>paraphrase your answer</u> by saying: *Yes, I <u>love</u> it. In fact, I <u>have</u> <u>enjoyed reading</u>. I <u>have been reading</u> mystery novels when I <u>was</u> a teenager.* (I used present, present perfect, present perfect continuous in my answer).

Let me give you another example here.

If they ask you *"what do you do in your free time?"*

You should <u>paraphrase your answer</u> by saying: *"In my leisure time/ in my spare time, I love to play games…"*

Or you can say *"when I am not working, I like to read books."*

Or you can say *"well, one of my hobbies is fishing."*

Paraphrasing statements about <u>favorite things/people</u>

If they ask you *"What's your favorite food to eat?"*

If you answer like this *"My favorite food definitely is X because…"*, you <u>will not get a high score</u> because you don't paraphrase.

Instead, you can use this structure ***"The X I love the most is…"*** to answer this question *"what's your favorite X…?"*

<u>Example:</u> *what's your favorite TV show?*

You can say: *The TV show I love the most is…*

What is your favorite place to visit?

You can say: *The city I love the most is New York…*

So you need to practice this structure, because if the examiner gives you a ***"favorite"*** question, then you know how to answer it excellently.

On the other hand, if they ask you *"What's your least favorite food to eat?"*

You would say: ***The X I love the least is…*** or ***I really dislike…***

"What's your least favorite food to eat?

You can say: *Well, the food I love the least is Kimchi, I generally don't like Korean food….*

Synonyms for Like and Dislike to paraphrase the questions:

LIKE:

Like, to be keen on, to be fond of, to be captivated by, to be fascinated by, to be tempted by, fancy, to be attracted to, to be passionate about.

DISLIKE:

Dislike, to be not keen on, to be not fond of, detest, hate, loathe, can't stand, can't bear, to be not captivated by.

Summary: You will not get a high score (7.0+) if you don't paraphrase your answer. You have to do it. You might be going to be slow at first. I know this, but the more you practice your paraphrasing, the easier it will get. You will be programmed like a computer.

Comparison: You can answer the question by using **comparison language**. Comparison language is so useful. This is something the examiner is expecting you to be able to do. They want you to be able to compare things. **What to compare?** Compare what you want, many things you can compare.

Do you like to read? Compare what you like to read with what you don't like to read. Compare what you like to read now with what you used to like to read when you were a child.

Compare what you like to read now with what you would like to read in the future.

Compare what you like to read with what your friends/your parents/people in your country like to read.

If the examiner gives you a question with one to two choices. They are inviting you to do something, they are hoping that you will be giving them a certain kind of language.

- *Would you rather own a dog or a cat as a pet?*

- *Do you prefer reading books or magazines?*
- *Do you like eating fast food or traditional food?*

First of all, you are going to PARAPHRASE. If they ask you *"Would you rather…?"*, you are going to answer *"I would prefer to…"*

Example: *Would you rather own a dog or a cat as a pet?*

Your answer should be *"I would prefer to own a dog/ I would prefer to own a cat."*

If they ask you *"Would you prefer to own a dog or a cat as a pet?"*

Your answer should be *"I would rather own a dog/ I would rather own a cat."*

Always note that comparison language is the thing that the examiner really wants you to do in your speaking. I promise to you that if you want to get a high score in the exam, you need to be able to compare. They want you to be able to *compare*. Also, they need you to use *non-defining relative clauses*, *dependent clauses*, and make sure that each sentence should have a purpose.

If this, then…however if this, then…

Given the option, I would prefer to…

My preference would be…..

PRACTICE:

Would you rather go to the movie or sing karaoke on Friday night?

STEP 1: You can start your answer by saying something that is generally true about both things.

- *Well, both of them are fun activities.*
- *Well, both of them are things that I really like to do.*
- *Well, both of those activities are things that my friends and I really love.*

STEP 2: Then you can start describing more details (positive and negative) about the two things using comparison structures:

Would you rather own a dog or a cat as a pet?

Both of them are really fun. However *(now you start talking about one of them)* dogs have <u>more personality</u> and are very loyal *(positive)*. But, they can <u>require more time</u> and a bigger home to take care of them properly *(negative)*. Cats, on the other hand do not need <u>as much space as</u> dogs *(positive)*. Also, they are <u>much more independent</u> *(positive)*. However, they can be <u>less friendly than</u> dogs *(negative)*.

STEP 3: Making your choice:

Given the option (what I am doing here is signaling that <u>I am making my choice</u>) I <u>would prefer</u> to have a dog because they are easier to have a strong relationship with.

Adjectives: you can use adjectives in your answer to describe things or people. Be sure to use adjectives with proper forms **"V-ED"** or **"V-ING"** exactly.

V-ED adjective: is used for the person or the thing <u>doing a feeling</u>.

V-ING adjective: is used for the thing <u>causing the feeling</u>.

- <u>Example 1:</u> You are at the theater. When you are watching the movie, someone who is sitting next to you is talking. They are *annoying*. That's why you feel *annoyed*.

- <u>Example 2:</u> When you go to the beach. The beach is so *relaxing*. That's why you feel so *relaxed*.

- <u>Example 3:</u> I was very *excited* because the movie was so *exciting*.

- <u>Example 4:</u> I wasn't *bored* because the movie was so *exciting*.

Remember to explain your adjectives. <u>Don't leave</u> these adjectives <u>unclear</u>. You should explain them by answering the question **"why?"** and <u>giving examples</u>.

Why A better than B?

Why was the movie so interesting?

Relative Clauses/ Relative Pronouns: you can use relative clauses or relative pronouns and past participle to add specific details in your answer. For example:

*"I really like jumping into the river. This is a lot of fun." **"This"** is a* relative pronoun.

You can make this sentence by using a relative clause *"I really like jumping into the river, which is a lot of fun."*

- *I like people who give me money.*

- *I like activities that are healthy.*

- *I really like people who give me money.*

- *These people are very friendly and I love them.*

- *Of all his friends, I am the one who he knows he can rely on.*

Try to give extra information by using relative clauses extremely flexible. We use relative clauses for part 1, part 2, part 3 speaking and even for task 1 and task 2 writing.

Number 3: Is the question about you or the question about other people?

If the examiner asks you *"do you like to read?"* or *"do you enjoy shopping?"* they are asking about you.

If the examiner asks you *"why do people enjoy reading?"* or *"why do people enjoy shopping?"*, they are not asking about you, they are asking about the people in general.

Be sure if they ask you *"do you like to read?"*

Again, you **shouldn't** say like this: *yes, reading is very popular, a lot of people like to read because it's so relaxing and helps them build their knowledge, so people read in their free time quite a lot....*

How is the grammar in the answer? The grammar is great. How is the vocabulary? The vocabulary is great. Unfortunately, I don't know if you don't understand the question or if you don't have the ability to answer in a proper way because you lack English skills. The examiner asked the question about you, and you answered the question about people in general. That's a problem. Be sure you got it.

Number 4: Is the question open or closed?

+ **Closed questions** are the ones that you can answer with *"yes"* or *"no"* or *"it depends"*

Example: *Do you enjoy watching television?*

+ **Open question** are the ones that you do not answer with *"yes"* or *"no"* or *"it depends"*

Example: *Why do people like watching television?*

This is a big difference because if they ask you about a closed question, you will give **a yes/no answer.**

Number 5: **Start and end your answer with confidence:** answer the question, show something or some things about your English ability and stop talking and let them ask you another question. Do not make your part 1 speaking answers too long. Don't do it, the examiner will get frustrated. They have questions that are designed to get different responses from you.

If they ask you *"do you like to read?"*

Don't answer the question too long like this *"yes, I love reading and I really enjoy reading mystery novels. A lot of people don't like mystery novels, but I really love them. When I was a child, I really loved reading comic books; back then I really love to read bad man."*

So please well prepare and focus on how to answer different types of IELTS questions. Plan and practice ways to answer questions clearly and fluently. Be specific about what you are studying, focus on something and practice regularly. Then, in the exam, be disciplined and stick with your plan. Know what you want to say and how you want to say it. Then you will easily get a high score in your part 1 speaking.

Number 7: **Develop good habits.** You should study many times a week, but only for 5-10 minutes for each time. Research has proved that this is the best way to master vocabulary and phrases. Try to avoid long study sessions only once a week. Practice whenever you have some free time, set small goals, and, if you do this regularly, you will make great improvements.

Number 8: There are some essential topics you must be prepared to discuss: your favorites (food, books, films, TV shows, personal item, website, etc.)...people in your life (family, friends, teachers, neighbors)...activities (hobbies, exercise, what you do on holidays, memories of past and plans for future), places (where you live, where you might like to live, places to visit, etc), and things (devices and gadgets you use every day, presents you have given or received, valuable and cherished objects).

Number 9: **Relax and be natural.**

FLUENCY MARKERS

What are fluency markers (discourse markers)?

Fluency markers are words or phrases that native speakers use to make their speaking sound more natural, smoother and clearer. We use these words or phrases to signal information.

You will not get a high score in the speaking test, part 1, part 2, or part 3 if you don't learn how to signal your answers, how to combine and link your sentences together. What you are seeing below are great examples that involve the fluency markers using different time expressions as well as different verb forms. I don't just use past simple, I use past continuous, and present perfect that we will need to do in the speaking test.

One of the fluency markers we've already talked about is "however". When you hear *"however"*, you know that will be signaling, changing about something.

For example: *Vietnam is really hot, and sometimes it rains which is very convenient.* ***However***…(now what I am saying about Vietnam, something positive or something negative?)

Something positive because you know when we are saying something…***however***…we will be signaling or we will be talking about something different.

My friends really love to go to the movie on Friday night. ***However,***…(I could be talking something they don't like to do like *"My friends really love to go to the movie on Friday night. However, they hate singing karaoke."*

So we can use these words to signal a lot of information. Practice using these fluency markers, then it will become your habit.

Let's talk about other fluency markers.

1. To be honest/ I'm afraid/ honestly: these are what we call softening phrases. We use these phrases to be more polite when we get a negative answer, or to signal that we are going to give a negative answer or you are not proud of what you will say.

Examples: *Do you enjoy reading?*

- *To be honest*, I don't really like reading.
- *Honestly*, I don't like reading very much.
- *I'm afraid*, I don't like it very much.

You are Japanese. How do you feel if you ask someone *"do you like Japanese food?"* and they say *"I don't like it"* Does that sound a bit rude? Yes, it sounds quite harsh. So you need to be more gentle with your negative answers or when you are not proud of something.

So it will sound better if you say *"honestly, I don't like Japanese food very much"*

However, what if I ask you *"do you smoke cigarettes?"*

Can you say *"To be honest, I don't smoke"*. Is it something you should feel ashamed of? **No**, you should be proud that you are not a smoker. Something like that, even though the answer is no, you don't really need to get the fluency marker *"To be honest/ I'm afraid/ honestly"* in this case.

2. Fortunately/ unfortunately: these are really great and easy-to-use words that students don't practice enough. They don't use them enough. These words are powerful and easy. We use these words to signal a positive or negative situation or condition, and we can use them in a combination. You can talk about the negative, and then, fortunately, a positive; or a positive, unfortunately, a negative.

Example 1: I remember it rained heavily that day (a negative). ***Fortunately***, I had my umbrella with me (a positive).

Example 2: My mother cooks for me every day (a positive). ***Unfortunately***, she's not a very good cook (a negative).

So, we can use these things in a combination.

You should practice using fluency markers in a combination with one another.

Example 3: *Do you enjoy reading?*

To be honest, *I'm not really keen on reading books.* **Unfortunately**, *I'm in university and my professor requires a lot of reading.*

So I just answer the question and I use two fluency markers. It's really helpful to make your speaking become more organized.

3. Actually/ In fact /As a matter of fact: We use these words to add details.

Example: *Do you enjoy reading?*

To be honest, I don't like to read very much. Unfortunately, I'm in university right now, and my professor gives me a lot of reading assignments. In fact, tonight I will have to read about 40 pages…

Ok. That works. Again, you should use all these fluency markers in a combination because that will help you get a better speaking score.

Actually: This can be used as a softening phrase. If I ask my girlfriend *"baby, do you love me?"* she says *"actually, you are not handsome, so I don't love you."*

4. However/ but: these words are used to signal a different idea or opinion. That could be a difference between now and in the past; or a difference between now and the future.

Example 1: *Do you enjoy traveling?*

Well, I love traveling. Unfortunately, I'm quite busy right now, so I haven't had a chance to go anywhere, **but** *I'm planning to travel to Thailand during Tet holiday.*

Example 2: *Going to the beach is a lot of fun.* **However**, *I would rather explore a big city.*

5. I suppose /I guess: These words are used to indicate a speculation. Speculation basically means *a guess*.

When you answer the question by using phrases *"I suppose or I guess"*, what you are showing the listener is that you do not know the exact answer, but you are trying very hard to give the best guess.

Example 1: *What's the population of Ho Chi Minh City?*

You can say something like: *that's a good question, I really don't know, but* ***I guess/suppose*** *it's about ten million people.*

Example 2: *What's the best university in the United States?*

You can say something like: *I* ***suppose*** *it's the Harvard University.*

6. Supposedly/ supposed to be: These words are called stereotype language.

What is a **stereotype**?

A stereotype is something that you have heard is true, but you do not know because you have not experienced it.

Example: *There are a lot of guns, violence in America.*

If you have never been to America, you **should not** say *"America is a violent country"* because you have never been there. Instead, you should say: *America is supposed to be a very violent country.*

Or: *some people say that living in New York is very enjoyable.*

7. I've heard (that) / some people say (that)

Use to express what you have heard to be true, but do not know by yourself, because you have not experienced it.

Vietnamese food is supposed to be delicious. I've heard (that) Vietnamese food is delicious.

TIME AND FREQUENCY EXPRESSIONS

1. Nowadays/ these days: We use these words for current actions and habits.

Example: *Do you enjoy watching television?*

Yes, I love watching television. Unfortunately, I don't have a lot of free time. Nowadays, I am doing a lot of studying at the university and I don't have a chance to watch my favorite programs.

Or: …..*Nowadays, I often watch cartoons. I especially like Tom & Jerry.*

2. Used to + Verb: We use this structure to talk about past actions and habits.

- *I used to go swimming with my friends.*
- *I used to yell at my coworkers.*

3. When I was X: we use this structure to talk about past actions and habits.

- *When I was a university student, I used to meet my friends for coffee every morning before class.*
- *I used to go to the library when I was in high school.*
- *I used to cook for my brother when I was a teenager.*

4. Adverbs of Frequency: We use adverbs of frequency *Never… Seldom/ rarely/ hardly ever… Sometimes… Often/ Frequently/ Nearly always …Usually/ typically/ normally… Always* to tell how often something is done

- *I never feel bored when I talk with him.*
- *I seldom/ rarely/ hardly ever go swimming on Sunday morning.*

- I *often* go to the university canteen to eat with my friends.

- I *usually* go to bed by 11 p.m.

5. Adverbs of Infrequency: *Every once in a while / Every so often / Every now and then / Every now and again.* Use in place of "sometimes and seldom"

- *Every once in a while* I play sports on the weekend.

- I play golf *every so often*.

- *Every now and then* we stay in bed all day and watch cartoons.

6. Concession and contrast: something is true; however, something else is true. We use this a lot. This is a massively useful structure because we use this structure a lot for part 1, part 2, part 3 speaking and task 2 writing.

Is watching TV popular in your country?

Teenagers and little children really enjoy watching television. However, the elderly prefer reading the newspaper.

Do you like food from other countries?

Well, food from other places is very delicious. However, I prefer eating food from Vietnam.

ADVERBIALS FOR GIVING OPINIONS

1. Personally: you are only giving your own opinion about something.

Personally, I don't think organized social events are very important.

2. Frankly/to be frank: you are saying something direct and honest.

Frankly/ to be frank, I don't like Korean food.

3. Typically: this situation is usually true or this is what usually happens.

4. Obviously/ clearly: a fact can be easily noticed or understood.

Obviously, the first aim of primary education is to teach students basic literacy skills.

5. Predictably/ inevitably: this situation was expected or certain to happen.

Predictably, most people find exams are stressful.

6. Inevitably/surprisingly: this situation was unexpected.

Surprisingly, ability is usually judged by exam results.

QUESTIONS ABOUT OTHER PEOPLE:

Quantities of people: *nearly everyone, almost everybody, the (vast) majority of + types of people, most + types of people, a large percentage of + types of people, some + types of people, a few + types of people, a handful of + types of people.*

Phrases of habit (showing that you are talking about a group): *as a rule, tend to, generally speaking.*

Types of people - ages: *young adults, people who are older, students, people who love animals,*

Types of people - behavior: *energetic people, sad people/ people who are sad, people with a sense of humor, lazy people, sporty people, religious people...*

Adjectives of evaluation (what we think about something): *thrilling, relaxing, interesting, fascinating, stimulating, exciting, inspiring, etc.*

USEFUL STRUCTURES:

S + believe/find something + Adjective

- *They find comic books boring.*

- *I find it exciting/wonderful.*

- *I find it delicious.*

- *As a rule, most teenage boys find videos games very exciting.*

Is watching cartoon a popular hobby in your country?

Yes, most children tend to watch animation. They are really keen on Tom & Jerry. Personally, I don't really like these shows. I find them a bit boring.

Why do some people enjoy horror films?

- *Who enjoys horror films?*

- *Why do they enjoy horror films?*

Using <u>adjectives</u> and <u>explanations for adjectives</u>: ….*they find horror films really thrilling. However, not many elderly like this genre because they tend to find them really disgusting.*

Do people in your country enjoy fast food?

- *Who enjoys fast food?* (Teenagers, young adults)

- *Why do they enjoy fast food?*

HIGH-SCORE VOCABULARY

Instead of saying *"I was very afraid"*, you can say *"I was terrified"*. It's much better when it comes to vocabulary.

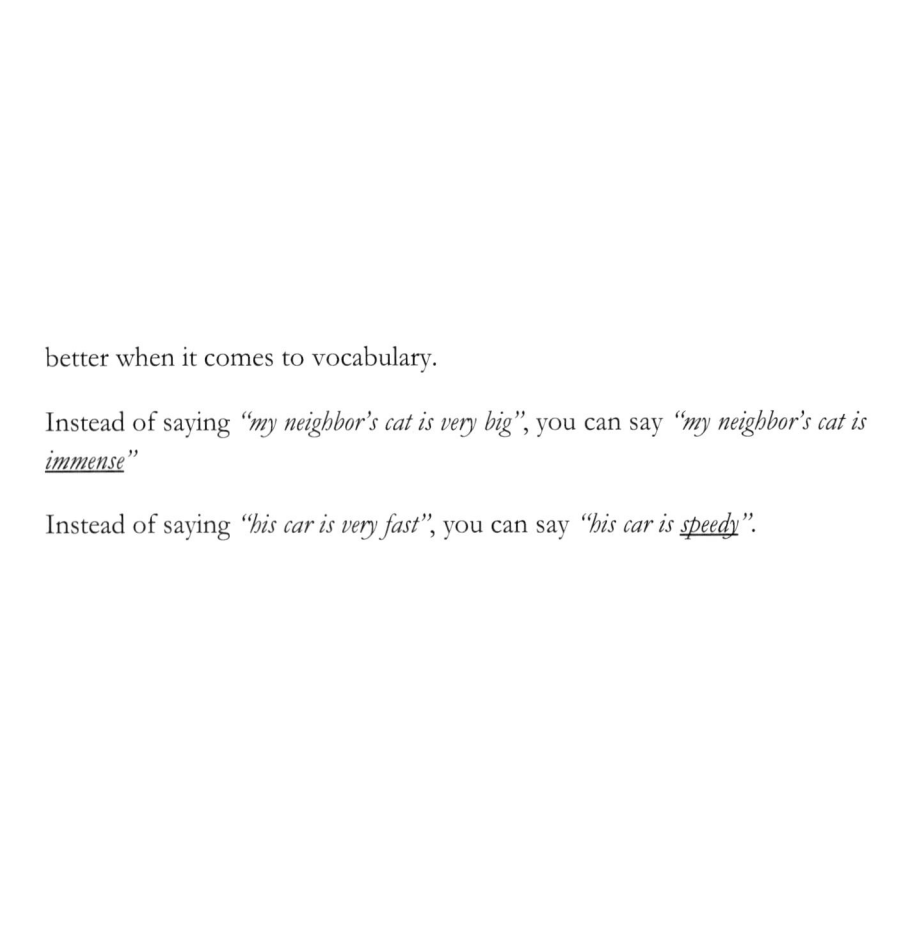

Instead of saying *"my neighbor's cat is very big"*, you can say *"my neighbor's cat is <u>immense</u>"*

Instead of saying *"his car is very fast"*, you can say *"his car is <u>speedy</u>"*.

PART 1 SPEAKING PRACTICE

QUESTIONS ABOUT WHERE YOU ARE LIVING

What kind of town or city are you living in at the moment?

You might say: *I live in a residential area in a highly populated city.*

Extend your answer: *I live in a big city. Actually, I live in a south side of Ho Chi Minh City. It's a residential area near a busy intersection.* (Try to focus on *place language*, and *prepositions*, then you will get a high score.)

How long do you live here? *I have lived here/I have been living here for about 5 years* (present perfect or present perfect continuous).

Or you can use the structure "since"

- *I have lived here/I have been living here since I started university.*

- *I have lived here/I have been living here since I began my job 2 years ago.*

QUESTIONS ABOUT ENTERTAINMENT: You can say something like *go shopping, drink coffee, singing karaoke, play sports, etc.*

You need to use a verb. You can talk about what you do, and you can talk about what other people do. That's is a great opportunity for you to show your vocabulary.

You can answer: *As a rule, young people in my neighborhood.../ As a rule, the young people where I live usually sing karaoke, drink a lot of beer, and ride a motorbike. However, the elderly tend to prefer to watch horror films.*

How would you describe the people who live there? (Using adjectives)

They are nice, friendly, supportive...

What you like most about living there? (Using superlatives)

- *The thing I love the most is…*

- *My favorite thing about Sydney is…*

- *I really love…*

- *What I really love is…*

What is your least favorite thing? (Using superlatives)

- *The thing I dislike the most is….*

- *Well, I really hate…*

- *The thing I really hate is…*

ADJECTIVES THAT ARE USED TO DESCRIBE PLACES:

- *Wild = remote*

- *My home is in the middle of nowhere (idiom) = very rural.*

- *It's off the beaten track: a place where people don't normally go/ a place is remote/ unusual area.*

- *Exciting = vibrant*

- *Friendly place = welcoming place = hospitable place*

- *A busy area = a crowded/ bustling/ hustle and bustle urban area.*

- *A dull place = not a very exciting place = a boring place*

- *A deserted place = an empty place (nobody around)*

- *Relaxing place = the place is very relaxing.*

QUESTIONS ABOUT MUSIC:

What type of music do you like most?

You might say: *My favorite style is jazz (***don't repeat** *the word "music" by saying*

~~my favorite type of music is~~) mainly because it's so relaxing after a stressful day at work.

Or: I am <u>a huge fan of</u> jazz. Actually, I will drive *(simple future)* to a club tonight *(when)* to listen to *(why)* a famous jazz guitarist *(who)*.

Or: I am <u>a huge fan of</u> jazz. Actually, I will be driving *(future continuous)* to a club tonight *(when)* to listen to *(why)* a famous jazz guitarist *(who)*.

We use **future continuous** to talk about something <u>in progress at a certain time</u>. With future continuous, you <u>need a time in the future</u>.

Next year I <u>will be studying</u> in London.

Two weeks from now, I <u>will be flying</u> home for Tet holiday.

We use **future perfect** to talk about <u>a completed action in the future</u>.

Luckily, by the end of the summer, my favorite band <u>will have played</u>.

I am <u>a huge fan of</u> Vietnamese food.

We can use various verb tenses in the answer: Last night, I <u>felt asleep</u> *(paste tense)* while I <u>was listening</u> *(paste continuous)* to music on my ear phones *(two verb forms in one sentence)*

How often did you play sports when you were young?

Back then, I used to meet my friends *(who)* for football matches *(why)* a few times a month *(how often)*.

What do you do on the weekend?

Answer 1: *My favorite type of music is Jazz. In fact, I love playing guitar (what) with my friends (who) in my bedroom (where) on the weekends (when). Sadly, I'm terrible (how), but I find it relaxing (why) (why I play guitar).*

Answer 2: *In fact, my father who shares his collection of music with me (what) when I was a teen (when). I love sitting in the living room (where) and relaxing while listening to his collection on my headphone (how).*

Answer 3: *Honestly, <u>my friends are very keen on</u> playing sports <u>but I prefer to</u> play guitars*

Do people in your country enjoy eating fast food?

Note: This is a question <u>not about you</u>, it's <u>about other people</u>.

Answer 1: *Yes, many of them do, especially teens. They are fans of cheese burger....*

Answer 2: *It depends, many Vietnamese teens like cheese burgers, but not a lot of them like KFC (something they do, something they don't).*

PREFERENCE QUESTIONS

What are preference questions?

Preference questions <u>always give you choice</u> *(would you rather do this or would you rather do that? do you prefer to do this or do you prefer to do that? do you like to do this or do you like to do that?)*

<u>Example:</u> *Would you rather see a romantic film or comedy?*

As a rule, with these questions, the examiner wants you to <u>talk about both things</u>. They are signaling to you that if they give you those types of question, they want you to talk about both things, they want you to <u>compare by using comparison structures</u>. You should do a couple of things here:

Would you rather own a dog or a cat as a pet?

STEP 1: You can start your answer by saying something that is <u>generally true about both things.</u>

Well, both of them are really fun.

STEP 2: Then you can start <u>describing more details</u> (positive and negative) about the two things <u>using comparison structures</u>:

However (now you start talking about one of them) dogs have <u>more personality</u> and are very loyal (positive). But, they can <u>require more time</u> and a bigger home to take care of them properly (negative). Cats, on the other hand, do not need <u>as much space as</u> dogs (positive). Also, they are <u>much more independent</u> (positive). However, they can be <u>less friendly than</u> dogs (negative).

STEP 3: Making your choice:

Given the option (what I am doing here is signaling that I am making my choice) I <u>would prefer</u> to have a dog because they are easier to have a strong relationship with.

Note: in order to get a high score in the speaking test, you have to <u>paraphrase</u> the question.

If they say *"would you rather eat bananas or apples?"*

You should say: *I'd prefer to eat apples* or *I'd prefer to eat bananas*.

If they say *"would you rather"*, you should say *"I would prefer"*

If they ask you *"would you prefer to eat bananas or apples?"*

You should say *"I would rather eat apples"*

PART 1 SPEAKING MODEL ANSWERS

"WORK" TOPIC

Do you work or are you a student?

Answer: *I am studying and working at the same time. Before I came to France, I was working as an engineer, but at the moment I'm studying French because I hope to do a Master's here.*

Do you like your job?

Answer: *well, generally speaking, I really enjoy my job simply because it's very rewarding to be able to help people every day. It also helps me boost my people skills, expand my social network and give me a financial security.*

Do you like your study?

Answer: *Yes, I really love studying law, but my real aim is to do a Master's and then look for a job in an international law firm.*

What do you like about your job?

Answer: *Frankly, I love everything about my current job. But, I think the best part of it is that I could travel and discover places that I have never been to.*

Is there anything you don't like about your job?

Answer: *Generally speaking, I enjoy my job. The only thing I am not so fond of is the salary; it's not good enough for me to enjoy my life. I wish my boss would give me a pay rise next month.*

Would you like to change your job in the future?

Answer: *I don't want to get stuck at the job that I am working now. I am still young, so 1 want to learn as much as I can. Moreover, I would like to be my own boss, so I'm planning to run my own business next year.*

"HOME TOWN" TOPIC

Where are you from? Where is your hometown?

Answer: *I'm from Ho Chi Minh, which is a city in the south of Vietnam.*

Do you like your home town? (Why?)

Answer: *Yes, I like living in Ho Chi Minh City mainly because it's where most of my friends and family members live, and because there are a lot of activities to do here. The only thing I don't like is the traffic; it's nearly always crowded and noisy.*

Would you prefer to live somewhere else? (Why?)

Answer: *For now, I'm happy living here. But at some point when I get old, I'd probably like to live in a place with a warmer climate, and many beautiful natural landscapes including beaches.*

Is your hometown suitable for young people to live in?

Answer: *Definitely yes, Ho Chi Minh City is a perfect place for young people to live in simply because it has lots of things for young generation to enjoy, such as sports facilities, gyms, schools, hospitals, public transport, and even leisure facilities.*

MUSIC TOPIC

Do you like music?

Answer: *Definitely yes. Music is my cup of tea. I love pop, hip hop, rock, and classical music mainly because it can cheer me up greatly when I feel bored or tired. I usually listen to music from my earphones when I'm traveling from place to place.*

Somebody's cup of tea: means what somebody likes or is interested in.

How often do you usually listen to music?

Answer: *Almost every day. Normally, I listen to music whenever I feel bored or depressed. I have favorite different playlists that can help me get into a particular mood whenever I feel down. Also, I like listening to music when I can't go to sleep, I like to listen to some light music to calm myself down.*

What kinds of music do you like?

Answer: *When it comes to music, yes, I am a big fan of all types of films, such as pop,* hip hop, rock, and classical music. I love listening to music simply because it can cheer myself up/ amuse myself/ relax myself/ release my pressure.

"FILM TOPIC"

Do you like watching films?

Answer: *Absolutely yes, I enjoy watching all types of films, such as romance, action, comedy, sci-fi, and cartoon. Normally when I want to relax, or have some fun I am really keen on watching films at cinemas since it has a better atmosphere with better sounds and visual effects.*

What kinds of films do you like best?/ What's your favorite film?

Answer: *Comedies are my favorite kinds of films. I love this genre simply because it can make me laugh and amuse myself when I feel bored.*

How often do you watch films?

Answer: *Normally, I enjoy watching films at cinemas when I am available during weekends. I like to watch a film with my friends so we could share a good time together, and afterward we will talk about the movie, whether we enjoyed it or not.*

Do you prefer to watch films in the cinema or at home?

Answer 1: *I prefer to watch movies at the cinema simply because it offers me an exciting atmosphere with better sound system and visual effects, so I could be more deeply involved in the film.*

Answer 2: *Mostly, I have a fancy for watching films at home simply because I can choose any movie I want to enjoy and I can watch it in my leisure time. Moreover, I can switch it off or switch channels when I feel uninterested. It is so convenient.*

OTHER TOPICS

Do you like dancing?

Answer: *Definitely yes, I am really keen on dancing. After a hard day at work, I often dance in a dance studio/ gym. I love dancing mainly because it is a great way to exercise my body and that keeps my body fit.*

Do you like traveling?

Answer: *Definitely yes, traveling is my most favorite. When I am free from study/when I am off work, I like to travel to different places with family members or my best friends. I love traveling simply because it brings me a lot of benefits. Particularly I can broaden my horizon. For example, I can meet different people from different places, try different food, and even learn different languages and cultures.*

Do You Prefer To Travel Alone Or With Others?

Answer 1: *Well, I definitely would rather travel with a group of friends simply because I would like to share many things, such as accommodation, transport and even laughter with my mates during the trip. It is much more fun and enjoyable. We can discover new things, try different foods, meet different people, and explore different places together. If I travel alone, I suppose I will be lonely and I may be even helpless when I am into trouble. So traveling in a group of friends is my preference.*

Answer 2: *I would prefer to travel alone. If I travel with a group, I may waste a lot time to wait for the entire group to be ready and complete everything. As a result, I will have less time to meet and make friends with different people when we eat and sightsee together. However, when I travel alone, I can plan the trip by myself, I will have more opportunities to discover new places, people and customs by myself. I can spend more time looking for and making friends with either other tourists or locals during my trip. Particularly, I will be able to decide to do whatever I like without depending on others.*

What is your favourite transport?

Answer: *Although there is a variety of transport choices such as buses, taxies, trains, subways, so on, my favorite way to travel is by plane, because it's quick and convenient, it is more punctual than other means of transport.*

How do you like to travel for a long-distance trip?

Answer: *Personally speaking, I would choose airplane as my priority for a long-distance trip simply because then it doesn't take me so long to get to my destination. Obviously, the airplane is the fastest way of transport, and I don't want to waste my valuable time on the trip.*

Do you have a driving license?

Answer: *Yes, I got my driving license since I was 20 years old, and I am planning to buy a new car for my travel next month.*

Do you prefer to be a driver or a passenger?

Answer: *Generally speaking, I would rather be a passenger mainly because it makes me less stressful and nervous. I don't need to pay my attention to the traffic, and I can spend time doing something like reading books or listening to music on my phone.*

What do you usually do on your holiday?

Answer: *I live far away from my parents so whenever it is time for holidays, normally I go back home to have a get-together with my family and best friends to celebrate holidays. Sometimes I prefer to travel to new places to broaden my horizons and enjoy breathtaking views.*

How often do you have holidays?

Answer: *Well, since I am a college student, so normally I enjoy two main periods when holidays last long, which are the summer holiday and Lunar new year holiday.*

Is it important to have holidays?

Answer: *Absolutely yes, holidays are really necessary for us to rest and give us a chance to do whatever we want to. For example, we can travel to different places to recharge our battery, or spend time with our loved ones so we could be revitalized and refreshed for study or work.*

What kind of places do you like to travel to?

Answer: *I love traveling to many places with beautiful natural landscapes and mountains that I've never explored before. However, I don't often have the opportunity to go to places like that due to lack of funds. So instead I would love to go to places where I can enjoy myself and do fun things together with my friends.*

Do you like doing sports?

Answer: *Certainly yes, I am a big fan of all sorts of sport, including football, badminton, jogging, cycling, and swimming. I find sports very beneficial in a variety of ways; for example, playing a sport can help me relax myself, lose weight and build my body. Playing sports is also a great way for me to socialize and strengthen teamwork spirit with my friends.*

Do you like reading?

Answer: *Absolutely yes, reading is really my cup of tea. I love to read all kinds of book including novels, newspapers, magazines, and textbooks. Obviously, reading is a part of my daily life simply because reading can help me broaden my horizon and keep up with the latest news and information.*

Do you read the newspaper?

Answer: *Certainly yes, but I prefer to read news online instead of paper form because it can help save the natural resources. Also, reading news on the website is totally free of charge. I can read news on my smart phone anytime, anywhere. It's very convenient.*

How often do you read books?

Answer: *Honestly, I'm a complete bookworm. I read all the time. I can read up to 20 books a week. I usually read comic books, but sometimes I change my reading habit slightly by reading books about science or nature. I prefer reading comic books simply because they are great way for me to relax myself and escape from my daily life routines, but I also enjoy science and nature books since they help me enrich my knowledge about the world I live in.*

Do you like shopping?

Answer: *Definitely yes, when talking about shopping, I must say that I am a really shopaholic. In my spare time, I like to go shopping at a supermarket for daily necessities, like cosmetics, skin care products, fashion stuff, and foods. I love shopping for a variety of reasons; for example, I can relax myself, meet my requirements on a daily basis and have an opportunity to catch up with the latest trend and fashion.*

Do you like collecting things?

Answer: *Yes, I'm really keen on collecting things. I have been collecting stamps and coins since I was a child, and I find this activity quite interesting. Collecting stamps and coins is very beneficial in a variety of ways for example it can help me acquire the knowledge of the world and cheer me up greatly when I feed bored.*

Is your family important to you?

Answer: *Absolutely yes, my family is the most important thing in my life. My parents gave me life, brought me up, and always supported me whenever I had difficulties. Without my family, I could not survive for more than three days and I don't think my life would be meaningful. Obviously, my family means everything to me.*

Are computers important to you?

Answer: *Certainly yes, computers are extremely necessary in my work and my study. Without computers, it would be inconvenient for me to complete my homework, do research online and even amuse myself since I am used to relaxing myself by playing computer games, listening to music, and chatting with my friends on computers every day.*

Do you prefer swimming in the sea or in a swimming pool?

Answer: *As a matter of fact, I would rather swim in a swimming pool than in the ocean simply because it's much safer, and I can avoid being attacked by a shark.*

Do you prefer to travel by bike or by bus?

Answer: *I would rather ride bicycle than travel by bus simply because it's so much more comfortable, convenient and even faster if I'm travelling during the rush hours and particularly I won't get stuck in traffic jams. Besides, cycling also provides me a great way to stay healthier as compared to other means of transport, including buses.*

Do you prefer eating at home or at restaurant? Do you prefer to eat out or eat at home?

Answer 1: *To be honest, I don't know how to cook and don't have someone to cook for me, so I would rather eat at restaurants than eat at home simply because restaurants usually offer me a more comfortable environment to eat and get together with my friends. In addition, I can also try a wider range of food that tastes more delicious than home-cooked meals like sushi, sashimi, and udon noodles. Furthermore, I don't need to worry about washing dishes when I finish eating. So, given the option, eating at restaurant is certainly my ideal choice.*

Answer 2: *I would rather eat at home simply because this can help enhance our relationships while we are preparing our meals and enjoying food together. What I mean is during our meals, we can talk, tell jokes and exchange feelings on our current affairs with each other so that we who are parents and children would have a chance to communicate with each other to keep track of what we are thinking and doing. In addition, eating at home is much cheaper than eating at restaurants, and certainly helps us save a lot of money. Furthermore, foods cooked at home will be more hygienic and guaranteed. So, given the option, I would prefer to eat at home.*

Which Do You Prefer, Saturday Or Sunday?

Answer: Personally speaking, I prefer Saturday rather than Sunday simply because I have more freedom and I find it more relaxing, and I can do freely what exactly I want to do. To be specific, I can have some drinks and stay out late at night with my friends without worrying about waking up early for work the next morning. In addition, that is also a great opportunity for us to relax, release pressure and strengthen our relationship after a hard week at work.

Do You Prefer Watching Sports Events On TV Or Live?

Answer: Personally speaking, I would rather watch sports on TV than attend a live game simply because it is more time-saving, convenient, enjoyable and less costly than watching sports live. To be specific, I can stay home and enjoy my favorite sports on TV without traveling a long distance from my home to the stadium and might face the congestion of the traffic of the stadiums. It's more comfortable and safer. More importantly, I may be able to see the game, the view of the players or the goal situations from all angles due to the close distance. Furthermore, when watching sports events on Tv, I can share my ideas and feelings with my family and friends; we can cheer our team up with a cup of beer, and enjoy our satisfaction and happiness.

So, given the option, I would prefer to watch sports on TV.

Do You Prefer Reading An Electronic Book Or A Real Book?

Answer: Personally, I would rather read electronic books mainly because it is more convenient. What I mean is electronic books are portable, easy to manage, and particularly free of charge. I don't have to carry a pile of books in my bag pack. What I need to do is just to turn on my kindle device and then start reading whatever I have in my mobile library.

Do you prefer shopping online or at a real store?

Answer: Personally, I would rather shop online simply because it is more convenient. What I mean is shopping online saves me a lot of time as well as money since I tend to have the opportunity to search for specific items with better prices and quality. In addition, I can order things online and get them delivered within the same day.

Do you prefer relaxing at home or outside?

Answer: *It depends, during the day I would rather be out of the house; therefore, I would like to go shopping or meet up with friends for playing sports or getting something to eat. However, in the evenings I tend to prefer to relax myself at home by surfing the internet or watching action films.*

Do you prefer writing letters or e-mails?

Answer: *Personally, I prefer communication by email simply because it is more economical, easier, cheaper and a lot quicker to communicate rather than writing a letter. For example, I am going to apply for a job at a Korean company overseas; if I sent a letter to the employer, it might take several weeks to arrive, and all my applications might be delayed. Furthermore, writing letters is more convenient since I can write to more than one person at the same time. Also, it's easy to attach photographs and documents to an email.*

All in all, I would rather write emails rather than write letters.

What do you like to do in your spare time?

Answer: *Well, there are a lot of activities I enjoy doing in my leisure time. I love swimming and I'm also quite into cycling. From time to time, I'm keen on reading books and taking photos. However, what I particularly enjoy doing is listening to classical music – it's so relaxing.*

What do you like to do in the evening?

Answer: *During the day I work really hard so in the evening, I would love to relax myself. I enjoy spending time with my family. I'm really keen on watching films, listening to rock music or reading books. From time to time, I prefer to go for a walk in the park with my wife.*

What do you like most about student life?

Answer: *The thing I particularly love about when I was a university student is the golden opportunity it gave me to enrich my knowledge and establish new relationships. To be specific, at university, I can not only increase my knowledge about my major, but I can also make lots of new friends.*

What is the best thing about your hometown?

Answer: *My hometown is Ha Noi, which is the capital city located in the north of*

Vietnam. The best thing I would like to talk about my hometown is its amazing history, architecture, local food and people. Ha Noi is the biggest city in Vietnam that is famous for many beautiful natural landscapes, tourist attractions and friendly people. But what I particularly value about my hometown is its local food. There are various types of food which are very delicious and easy to find out around the city.

LIST OF PART 1 SPEAKING QUESTIONS TO PRACTICE AT HOME

QUESTIONS ABOUT YOU:

1. What do you dislike about X?
2. How often do you do X?
3. What do you like most about X?
4. Do you prefer X to Y?
5. What do you usually/normally do?
6. What do you like to do (in your spare time)?
7. When was the first/last time you did X?
8. Did you ever learn to do X?
9. How would you improve X?
10. What do you want/hope to do (in the future)?

QUESTIONS ABOUT OTHER PEOPLE:

1. How has X changed?
2. How important is X?
3. Do people do/get enough X?
4. How can people find out about X?
5. Is X popular (in your country)?
6. Why do some people like X?
7. Is it difficult to do X?
8. Is X suitable for (types of people)?
9. What is the best time (of year) to do X?
10. Should people be given X?

WORK

1. What's your job?

2. Why did you choose that kind of work?

3. How long have you been doing it?

4. What is a typical day like at your work?

5. Are there things you don't like about it? What are they?

STUDYING

1. What subjects are you studying?

2. Why did you choose those subjects?

3. How long have you been studying them?

4. Do you enjoy them? Why?

5. What is the best thing about studying?

MOVIES

1. Do you enjoy going to see movies?
2. What is your favorite type of film?
3. When was the last time you went to the cinema? What did you see?
4. What do you think of people who talk during movies?
5. Are horror films popular in your country?
6. Are there any actors or actresses you admire?
7. On a date, would you rather see a romantic film or a comedy?
8. Do you download films from the Internet?
9. When would you prefer to watch a film at home rather than at a cinema?
10. What is the next film you want to see?

READING

1. Do you enjoy reading?
2. What do you usually like to read?
3. Do you prefer to read the news in print or online?
4. What did you like to read as child?
5. Do people in your country enjoy reading?
6. Do you often read comics? Why?
7. When was the last time you read a book?
8. What book would you recommend your friends read?

SPORTS

1. Do you enjoy playing sports? Which?
2. What sports do you like to watch on TV?
3. Which sports are popular in your country?
4. Are there any sports you don't like?
5. Is it important for a child to learn a sport?
6. Do you admire any famous athletes? Who?

TELEVISION

1. Do you like to watch TV? Why or why not?
2. What are your favorite programs?
3. Are there any shows that you don't like?
4. When do you usually watch TV?
5. Is watching TV a popular hobby for people in your country?
6. Why do people like watching TV?
7. How does watching a film on TV different from going to the cinema?
8. How do you feel about advertisements?
9. Do you use the TV to help you learn English? How?
10. What TV show from your country would you recommend to a foreigner?

FOOD AND COOKING

1. Do you enjoy cooking?
2. How often do you eat at restaurants?
3. What is your favorite food to eat?
4. What is a typical breakfast for you like?
5. Do you like food from other countries?
6. Did you eat breakfast this morning?
7. In your culture, are their special foods served during holidays?
8. What foods would you like to try but never have?
9. Is there a type of food you don't like or would never try?
10. Do you prefer to eat at home or at restaurants?
11. Are there foods you used to like, but no longer do?

TRAVELLING

1. Do you enjoy travelling? Why?
2. Where have you travelled?
3. Would you rather travel alone or with friends and family?
4. What do you dislike about travelling?
5. Describe how you prepare for a trip.
6. Do you prefer using a train or plane when you travel? Why?
7. Do people in your country enjoy travelling? Where do they usually go?
8. Where will you go on your next holiday?

MUSIC

1. Do you like music?

2. What kind of music do you like?

3. When do you usually listen to music?

4. What kind of music did you like when you were younger? What kind of music is popular in your country?

5. Do you play any musical instruments?

6. Do you wish you could play any musical instruments?

7. Which is your favorite instrument?

8. Can music change a person's mood?

9. How is music you listen to different from the music your parents listened to when they were young?

10. What makes a song "good"?

11. Do you prefer music that relaxes you or gives you energy?

12. Why do people like going to concerts?

OUTDOOR ACTIVITIES

1. What kind of outdoor activities do you enjoy?

2. Would you rather go camping in the woods or go to the beach?

3. Where do people in your country go to enjoy nature?

4. How important is it to enjoy natural beauty?

5. When was the last time you went to the beach or the mountains?

6. Describe how you prepare for a trip to the outdoors.

CITY AND COUNTRYSIDE QUESTIONS

1. Do you like living in a big city?

2. What do you like the most about city life?

3. What is your least favorite thing about living in a city?

4. What do children in your country do for fun in the countryside?

5. How does a vacation in a rural area different from one in the city?

6. What types of amenities are commonly found in small towns and villages in your country?

7. Would you prefer to live in a city or a village? Why?

8. What social problems did your hometown have when you were a child? Have these problems improved or gotten worse?

LIFESTYLE AND LEISURE QUESTIONS

1. What do you do in your free time?

2. Can you describe your typical day?

3. What do you like to do on holidays?

4. How often do visitors come to your home?

5. Do you like to read" books?

6. What is your favorite type of music?

7. Do you prefer warm or cool weather?

8. Is going to a gym popular in your country?

9. What is the best time of day for you to study?

10. Do you enjoy working in the garden?

11. When was the last time you cooked a meal?

12. Did you learn to play a musical instrument when you were younger?

13. How would you like to improve your lifestyle?

14. Do people in your country appreciate art?

PREFERENCES

1. Do you prefer watching TV or reading books?

2. Would you rather eat at home or in a restaurant?

3. How popular are comedies compared to horror films in your country?

4. Do your friends prefer to go out or stay at home on weekends?

5. Would you rather own a dog or a cat as a pet?

6. Do you prefer giving presentations or writing essays for school?

7. Would you like to visit Europe or the United States?

8. In your country, how popular are computer games compared to playing cards?

9. Would you rather get a laptop, a tablet, or a smart phone as a present?

ANIMALS

1. What is your favorite animal?

2. What was your favorite animal when you were a child?
3. Do you have a pet?
4. What animals do people keep as pets in your country?
5. Why do people keep pets?
6. Are there any animals which are symbols in your culture?
7. When was the last time you went to the zoo?
8. What are zoos like in your country?
9. Have you ever gone hunting?
10. Is hunting an important part of your country's culture?
11. Would you rather have a dog or a cat as a pet?
12. Would you like to own an exotic pet such as a snake or a tarantula?

CELL PHONES

1. How often do you use a cell phone every day?
2. Would your life be better or worse without a cell phone?
3. Do you ever send or receive text messages when you shouldn't?
4. Could you survive without a cell phone?
5. What are the worst things about cell phones?
6. What features do you look for in a cell phone?
7. Do you plan to buy a new phone?
8. How did you feel when you bought your first cell phone?

COMMUNICATION AND LANGUAGE

1. How long have you been studying English?

2. Have you studied any other languages?

3. Do you often practice another language with your friends?

4. What is the most difficult thing about learning a new language?

5. Would you rather use the Internet or a book to study a language?

6. Is your native language easy for a foreigner to learn?

EDUCATION

1. Are you currently in school? What do you study?

2. When do you usually do homework?

3. Do you enjoy studying in groups or alone? Why?

4. Is there a subject you have never studied but are interested in?

5. Who was your favorite teacher when you were a child?

6. What is your least favorite subject to study?

7. Does taking exams cause you to feel stressed?

8. How do you relieve stress when you are studying?

9. Describe your routine for doing homework.

10. Is a high-level of education valued in your country?

11. Were you involved in non-academic activities at school?

12. If you could go back to high school, what would you do differently?

13. How often do you ask a teacher for extra help?

14. What is the study environment like at your school's library?

FOOD AND COOKING

1. Do you enjoy cooking?

2. How often do you eat at restaurants?
3. What is your favorite food to eat?
4. What is a typical breakfast for you like?
5. Do you like food from other countries?
6. Did you eat breakfast this morning?
7. In your culture, are their special foods served during holidays?
8. What foods would you like to try but never have?
9. Is there a type of food you don't like or would never try?
10. Do you prefer to eat at home or at restaurants?
11. Are there foods you used to like, but no longer do?

GAMES

1. Do you enjoy playing games?
2. What sorts of games do you enjoy playing?
3. Do you prefer games where you work as a team or work alone?
4. What kinds of games did you enjoy as a child?
5. Are there any games that are traditionally popular in your country?
6. How often do you play computer games?
7. When was the last time you played a computer game?
8. What do you like about computer games? What do you dislike?

FAMILIES

1. Do you come from a large family?
2. When do you often spend time together?

3. Does your family prefer to stay home on the weekends or go out?

4. Would people in your country rather have a large or small family?

5. What special things did you do with your family as a child?

6. Do you ever practice English with a family member?

HEALTH

1. Are you a member of a health club?

2. What kinds of exercise do you do?

3. Who is the healthiest person in your family? What do they do to keep healthy?

4. Do you have a lot of stress?

5. What are some things that cause people to feel stress? What are some ways to deal with stress?

6. When was the last time you ate fast food?

7. Do you know someone who smokes? Do they plan on quitting?

8. Have you ever smoked cigarettes?

9. What disease frightens you the most? Why?

10. If you were ill, what would you do to feel healthy again?

11. What do you think of cosmetic surgery? Would you ever consider it?

FREE TIME AND HOBBIES

1. What do you like to do in your free time?

2. What hobbies did you have as a child?

3. Did your parents have any hobbies? Did you help them?

4. If you could try a new activity, what would it be?

5. Do you enjoy relaxing hobbies or exciting ones?

6. Do you have a special talent? What have you done to practice this special talent?

7. Is it better to do hobbies alone or with other people?

8. Why are hobbies important?

HOLIDAYS/ VACATIONS

1. When was the last time you went on a vacation?

2. Do you prefer- to visit familiar or new places when on a holiday?

3. Is travelling alone enjoyable for you?

4. Have you ever visited a foreign country? Where?

5. Where will you go on your next vacation?

6. If you could go anywhere, where would you go?

7. What are some popular tourist attractions in your country?

HOMETOWN

1. Where do you come from?

2. Can you tell me something about your hometown?

3. Is your hometown famous for anything?

4. What places should foreigners visit in your hometown? Why?

5. Is there anything you would like to change in your hometown?

6. What places do you like in your hometown best?

7. How has your hometown developed in the last 10 years?

8. What amenities does your town provide?

9. What are the main crops in your region?

10. What other industries are important for your hometown's economy?

1. 11 .When is the best time of year to visit your hometown?

HOUSEWORK

1. What types of household chores do you do?
2. Do you ever help with the cooking?
3. Is there a certain time that you do housework?
4. Are you good at any particular household task?
5. What is your least favorite chore to do?
6. If you could avoid doing a specific chore, what would it be?

THE INTERNET

1. How often do you use the Internet?
2. What was your first experience with the Internet like?
3. What do you mainly use it for?
4. Tell me about your favorite website.
5. Do you use Facebook or twitter?
6. What is your least favorite thing about the Internet?
7. Would you rather watch films online or at the cinema?
8. Do you like to access the Internet on your mobile phone?
9. What do you think about "blogging"?
10. Have you ever uploaded a video to Youtube.com?

MONEY

1. Are you good at saving money?
2. What do you usually spend your money on?
3. How often do you go shopping?
4. Do you ever use a credit card?
5. Would you rather shop at a mall or a small market?
6. What do you 4hink about online shopping?
7. When was the last time you shopped for clothing?
8. Is fashion important to you?
9. What is the most expensive thing you have ever bought?
10. How is shopping alone different from shopping with friends?
11. Tell me about your favorite shop.
12. Are there some shops that you refuse to spend money at? Why?

DESCRIBING HABITS

1. What do you like to cook?
2. What did you like to watch on TV when you were a child?
3. Where do you spend time with your friends?
4. What kind of clothes do you like to wear?
5. Do you ever do charity work?
6. How often do you read the newspaper?
7. When do you usually do housework?
8. What sports did you play when you were growing up?
9. Who do you practice English with?

10. Do you enjoy singing karaoke?

11. Which foods don't you like?

12. Did you help your mother with household tasks when you were a teenager?

COMPUTERS

1. How often do you use a computer?
2. What are your favorite things to do on a computer?
3. Do you enjoy playing computer games?
4. Did you have difficulties the first time you used a computer?
5. Does the computer ever distract you from completing important tasks?
6. What is your opinion regarding social networking sites?
7. Can you tell me about your favorite website?
8. Do you use a computer to study English? How?

FUTURE PLANS

1. Why are you taking the IELTS test?
2. What are you planning to do in the next five years?
3. What are you planning to do in the next ten years?
4. What is the first thing you will do when you arrive at the new place?

THE SEA

1. Have you ever made a journey by boat?
2. Is the seaside a popular destination for people in your country?

3. What do you think should be done to prevent pollution of the oceans?
4. Do you enjoy going to the beach?
5. When you go to the beach, what do you normally do?

MODERN LIFE

1. Is life in your country today very different from when your grandparents were your age?
2. What things are changing in your country at the moment? Do you think modern life is healthy?
3. Where do people from your country like to go on vacation?
4. Have you ever been abroad? Did you enjoy it?

WEATHER AND SEASONS

1. What seasons do you have in your country?
2. Which season do most people go away on holiday in your country? Why?
3. Which season do you like the most? Why?

CONCLUSION

Thank you again for downloading this book on *"IELTS Speaking Part 1 Strategies: The Ultimate Guide with Tips, Tricks and Practice on How to Get a Target Band Score of 8.0+ in 10 Minutes a Day."* and reading all the way to the end. I'm extremely grateful.

If you know of anyone else who may benefit from the useful strategies, structures, tips, Speaking Part 1 language in this book, please help me inform them of this book. I would greatly appreciate it.

Finally, if you enjoyed this book and feel that it has added value to your work and study in any way, please take a couple of minutes to share your thoughts and post a REVIEW on Amazon. Your feedback will help me to continue to write other books of IELTS topic that helps you get the best results. Furthermore, if you write a simple REVIEW with positive words for this book on Amazon, you can help hundreds or perhaps thousands of other readers who may want to improve their English speaking sounding like a native speaker. Like you, they worked hard for every penny they spend on books. With the information and recommendation you provide, they would be more likely to take action right away. We really look forward to reading your review.

Thanks again for your support and good luck!

If you enjoy my book, please write a POSITIVE REVIEW on Amazon.

-- Rachel Mitchell --

CHECK OUT OTHER BOOKS

Go here to check out other related books that might interest you:

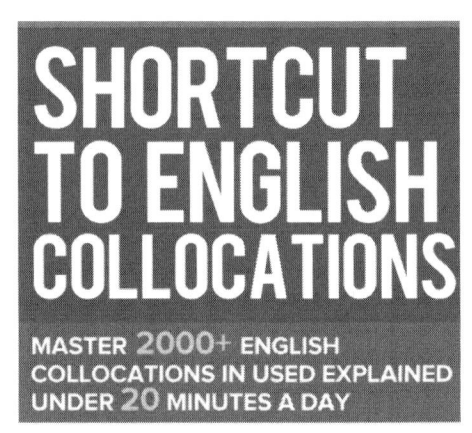

Shortcut To English Collocations: Master 2000+ English Collocations In Used Explained Under 20 Minutes A Day

https://www.amazon.com/dp/B06W2P6S22

IELTS Writing Task 1 + 2: The Ultimate Guide with Practice to Get a Target Band Score of 8.0+ In 10 Minutes a Day

https://www.amazon.com/dp/B075DFYPG6

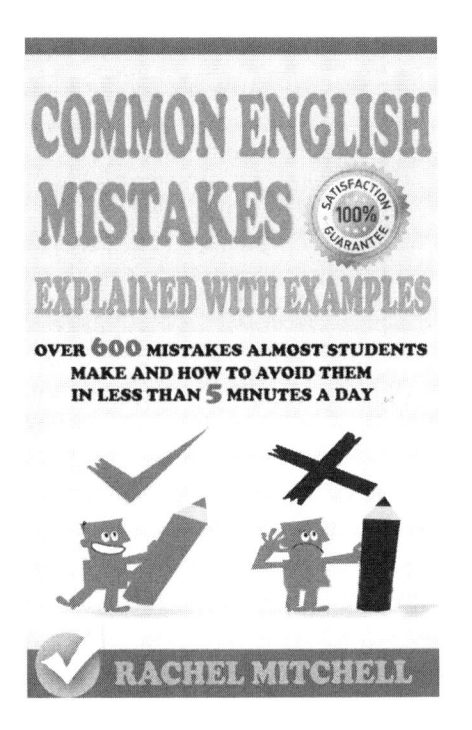

Common English Mistakes Explained With Examples: Over 600 Mistakes Almost Students Make and How to Avoid Them in Less Than 5 Minutes A Day

https://www.amazon.com/dp/B072PXVHNZ

Paraphrasing Strategies: 10 Simple Techniques For Effective Paraphrasing In 5 Minutes Or Less

https://www.amazon.com/dp/B071DFG27Q

Legal Vocabulary In Use: Master 600+ Essential Legal Terms And Phrases Explained In 10 Minutes A Day

http://www.amazon.com/dp/B01L0FKXPU

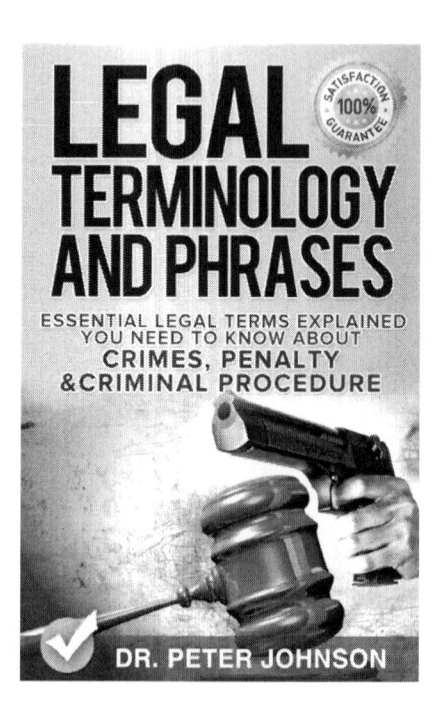

Legal Terminology And Phrases: Essential Legal Terms Explained
You Need To Know About Crimes, Penalty And Criminal Procedure

http://www.amazon.com/dp/B01L5EB54Y

Productivity Secrets For Students: The Ultimate Guide To Improve Your Mental Concentration, Kill Procrastination, Boost Memory And Maximize Productivity In Study

http://www.amazon.com/dp/B01JS52UT6

Daughter of Strife: 7 Techniques On How To Win Back Your Stubborn Teenage Daughter

https://www.amazon.com/dp/B01HS5E3V6

Parenting Teens With Love And Logic: A Survival Guide To Overcoming The Barriers Of Adolescence About Dating, Sex And Substance Abuse

https://www.amazon.com/dp/B01JQUTNPM

Understanding Men in Relationships: The Top 44 Irresistible Qualities Men Want In A Woman.

https://www.amazon.com/dp/B01MQWI11G

Printed in Great Britain
by Amazon